I ♥ CATS

Adamsmedia

Avon, Massachusetts

Published by
Adams Media, a division of F+W Media, Inc.
57 Littlefield Street, Avon, MA 02322. U.S.A.
www.adamsmedia.com

ISBN 10: 1-4405-8113-4
ISBN 13: 978-1-4405-8113-7
eISBN 10: 1-4405-8114-2
eISBN 13: 978-1-4405-8114-4

Printed in China.

10 9 8 7 6 5 4 3 2 1

Cover image © iStockphoto.com/Lise Gagne.

This book is available at quantity discounts for bulk purchases.
For information, please call 1-800-289-0963.

A group of kittens is called a "kindle."
That's probably because they are so
good at warming your heart!

Cats make fantastic hide-and-seek buddies. They can slink into such small crannies!

Cats take it easy by sleeping an average of thirteen hours a day. Looks like this cuddly kitty loves his laidback lifestyle!

Don't fault your cat for acting like a fussy princess during dinner. Since her jaws can only move up and down, it's easier for her to chew dainty cuisine.

Cats use their whiskers, in part, to let others know how they're feeling. How do you think this little guy feels?

Are those gray hairs I see?
On average, cats live up to fifteen years!

Cats clean themselves ⅓ of the time they're awake, so they're ready to snuggle at any moment.

When kittens chase their toys,
they're really honing their fierce
hunting skills for the future.

A cat's sense of sight is so keen that in a chaotic room, she can zero in on a floating spec of dust.

The first cat to take a trip to space was
French and named Félicette. Bien fait!

No wonder we're so emotionally attached to our sweet felines. We have identical regions in the brain responsible for emotions.

More than 40 percent of cats are ambidextrous. Too bad there's not a feline baseball league—they'd be real sluggers!

Cats dream of mice, milk, and your snuggles from as early as a week old. Can you blame them?

Cats must have a great appreciation for Mariah Carey! They can hear sounds up to two octaves higher than we can.

Truly one-of-a-kind, the Turkish Van doesn't mind frolicking in the water because his coat is completely water-resistant.

Dude, forget about those shades! Cats don't squint because of the sun—it's to show you that they're happy.

The wolf in *Little Red Riding Hood* might as well have been a kitten! Did you know that kittens have needle-sharp teeth for their first six months?

Male cats tend to be left-handed . . . err, -pawed.

Look at them go!
Domestic cats can scurry
as fast as 30 mph.

Keep the salt on the table for now—black cats aren't an omen of bad luck in all cultures. In fact, they are considered a sign of good fortune in the United Kingdom and Australia!

Female cats are more likely to be right-pawed. You heard it, ladies, right-pawed!

Return those night-vision goggles you just bought! A cat's vision requires six times less light than that of a human.

In the original Italian version of *Cinderella*, the Fairy Godmother was a cat. Now that wouldn't fare well for Jaq, Bruno, and Gus, would it?

Cats can sense your feelings, which is why they're such good listeners and roommates.

Cats can't taste sweetness,
but they can hear it in your voice.

Cats use their whiskers to measure the width of openings. Now, aren't they resourceful?

In the Middle Ages, cats got a bad rep for having their part in black magic. An undeserving reputation for such a crafty and majestic animal!

Purring doesn't just signify contentment—it's more of a plea to settle down next to them, whether they feel anxious, needy, or yes, simply happy!

It's not just farm animals that enjoy eating grass cats often munch on some to help their digestion.

She's not being scandalous—sniffing other cats is a way to say hello.

The smallest purebred cat is the
itty-bitty Singapura, often weighing
in at just 4 pounds!

Cats aren't always so cuddly. Wildcats are known to be very solitary and guarded.

Next time your cat gives you a nibble,
remember that wrestling and
"love-biting" is often a normal
part of feline playtime.

Though it may seem like they're head-butting you, knocking their head into your legs is a sign of affection.

Ever wonder why your cat conveniently chooses
to lounge directly on your laptop?
They can't get enough of the radiating heat.

Their ability to hunt rodents likely first drew humans to take cats as pets. Although, who could resist this adorable face?

Cats have dogs beat—
they can make more
than 100 different
sounds, while dogs only
make about ten.

Big and small, long-haired and short-haired: Cats come in all different adorable shapes and sizes. In fact, there are approximately forty different recognized breeds in the world.

Quite the hoity-toity eaters, cats prefer their food warm—too hot or cold might have them turning up their nose!

Cats keep their heads completely level
when chasing their prey . . . or, you know,
just their feisty mouse toy.

Talk about a full house—the world's largest litter included nineteen kittens!

My, what big ears you have! A cat's hearing is better than a dog's, meaning they're more likely to respond to your loving words.

It's confirmed! Cats are the world's most popular pets.

Ancient Egyptians worshipped a cat goddess named Bastet, which probably made that regal kitten purr!

Cats usually have twelve whiskers on each side of their nose—the better to feel your affection!

Forget man's best friend—a cat's brain is more
biologically similar to that of a human than that of
a dog, making them our ideal companion.

Charming and beautiful, the Persian is one of the oldest recognized cat breeds.

Don't be deceived by those big eyes—they're not just for looks. They're designed to help cats hunt at night.

It may seem sweet that she's chattering to the birds outside, but don't let it fool you—babbling is a reflex in anticipation of the hunt!

Don't bother asking this cutie if she wants to take a dip in the pool. Cats generally dislike being wet because it's just too chilly!

The heaviest cat on record weighed
in at more than 46 pounds.
That's a fat cat!

Cats are so graceful
and balanced thanks to
their long tails.

Their cuteness is ancient news: Cats have been domesticated for about 4,000 years!

Cats can rotate their ears 180 degrees to make sure that they can always hear their praise!

You know cats want to play when they roll back and forth on their back, like this tiny cutie, who just wants to have fun with you!

When hunting, cats place their back paws where their front paws stepped, making them harder to track. Who said dogs were the smarter pets?

Shipped in from Europe to help
with the pest problem, cats made
their American debut in the 1750s.

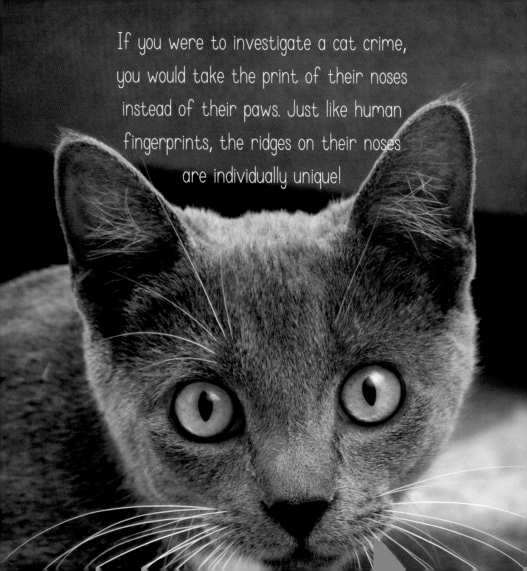

If you were to investigate a cat crime, you would take the print of their noses instead of their paws. Just like human fingerprints, the ridges on their noses are individually unique!

The oldest pet cat's ancestor links to the African wildcat Felis silvestris lybica. Now that's fierce!

Unlike dogs, cats are almost never intentionally bred.
They pick their own purr-fect soulmates!

Cats build a bond with their caretaker at an early age, so make sure you show your little guy lots of love!

Cats can be trained
to use the toilet.
Goodbye, litter box!

Many cats can develop a range of sounds and inflections in their meows to communicate just how much they care!

Female cats are known as "queens"—an appropriate title for her royal adorableness.

Commonly exceeding 20 pounds, the biggest cat breed is the Maine Coon. Although their kittens are larger than most, they're just as cute and cuddly as their friends!

They're not role-playing! Sitting in a position that resembles a roast turkey is a cat's way of showing you that he feels content and safe.

According to the APPA, there are nearly 20 million more pet cats than there are pet dogs in the United States.

The original breed name for this adorable Scottish Fold is Flops for—yup, you guessed it!—their floppy ears.

Now here's a gym partner anyone would envy! Cats only sweat through their paws, keeping them always looking fresh and beautiful.

"Slinky cat" isn't just a meaningless phrase. Cats are extremely flexible because of their loose-fitting vertebrae.

Ever wonder about the origin of the cat-stuck-in-the-tree scenario? Cats can't climb down headfirst because their claws all point in the same direction, which is why they often get stuck in high places.

Pucker up!
Cats hate citrus.

The Persian is the most popular pedigreed cat,
although you wouldn't guess their cool-cat status
from their sweet and down-to-earth personality.

Kittens are born after only nine weeks in the womb!
But don't worry, they come out ready to love you.

Odds are, your favorite feline weighs 8 to 11 pounds, just the right size for hugging!

Cats who interact with humans before eight weeks old make friendlier, cuddlier pets than those who have their first human interaction after ten weeks.

Cats gracefully land on their feet due to organs in the inner ear that sense where they are in a space.

The first cat show was held in London in 1871, where the winner ate plenty of celebratory fish 'n chips!

Purrr, it's cold up there!
Maine's state cat is,
appropriately, the Maine Coon.

Most litters include four to six kittens—
the more cuteness, the merrier!

Cats often signal their mood and intention through the movement of their tail. Sticking it straight up in the air is a welcoming greeting to friends.

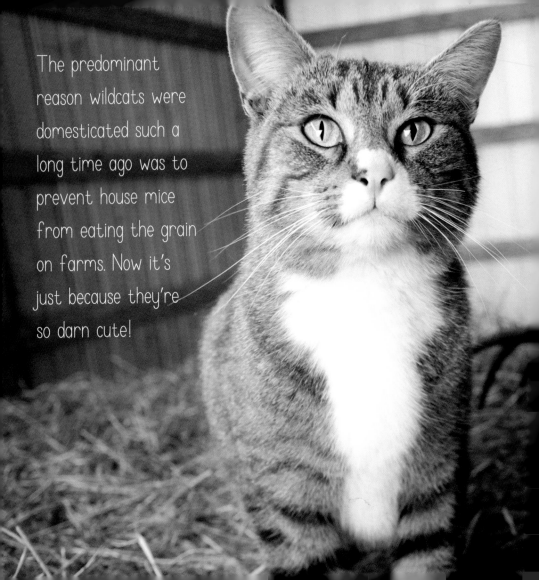

The predominant reason wildcats were domesticated such a long time ago was to prevent house mice from eating the grain on farms. Now it's just because they're so darn cute!

Cats' hearts beat almost twice as fast as humans' do. They probably love twice as much, too!

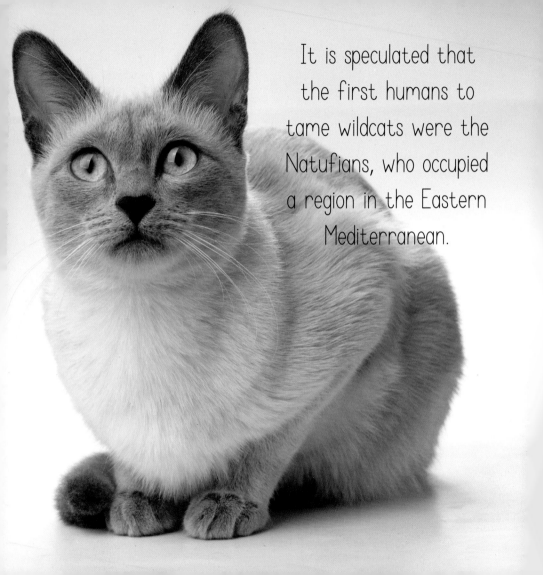

It is speculated that the first humans to tame wildcats were the Natufians, who occupied a region in the Eastern Mediterranean.

It's that cat instinct! Right out of the womb, kittens know how to meow and converse among themselves.

Cats living in warmer weather have more babies. Perhaps another reason to move south in the winter?

It's a compliment when they show their bellies. It's body language for, "I trust you. Now, pet me!"

They aren't boogying down when they wiggle their bums back and forth. They're positioning themselves to pounce!

No need to kick this habit—it's just too precious! Cats often massage soft surfaces before falling asleep—it's a leftover trait from when they would knead their mother's stomach for milk.

A male cat is called a "Tom," while a female is sometimes called a "Molly."

Mothers know best, often shooing away their male offspring just a few months after birth to avoid inbreeding.

Eyes are the windows into the soul, right? It's a sign of trust when cats close their eyes slowly while looking at you.

It's a bird, it's a plane—no, it's a ... cat! In one single bound, they can leap into your warm embrace.

There are 500 million adorable domesticated cats in the world. Make this cat 500 million and 1!

Isaac Newton gave us more than theories of motion and gravity. He also invented the pet door to stop his beloved cat Spithead from messing around with his experiments.

Your trash might be your cat's treasure. They love lounging in boxes because it gives them a sense of security.

Perhaps Abraham Lincoln is such a beloved president because he not only spoon-fed his son's cat, but also rescued three half-frozen kittens from a battlefield telegraph hut.

Don't go in for that high-five just yet. Cats raise one leg in the air to more easily clean themselves.

Don't ask your favorite feline for wardrobe help—cats only see in shades of blue and green.

You know they're feeling chilly
when they curl up in a perfect circle.
So help them out and cuddle!

No need to count twice:
Cats have five toes on their
front paws and only four
toes on their back paws.

Make way for this future basketball player! Cats can reach up to five times their own height per jump.

Who says bigger is better? Deemed the smallest cat in the world, Tinker Toy, a Himalayan–Persian, measured only $2\frac{3}{4}$ inches tall and $7\frac{1}{2}$ inches long as an adult!

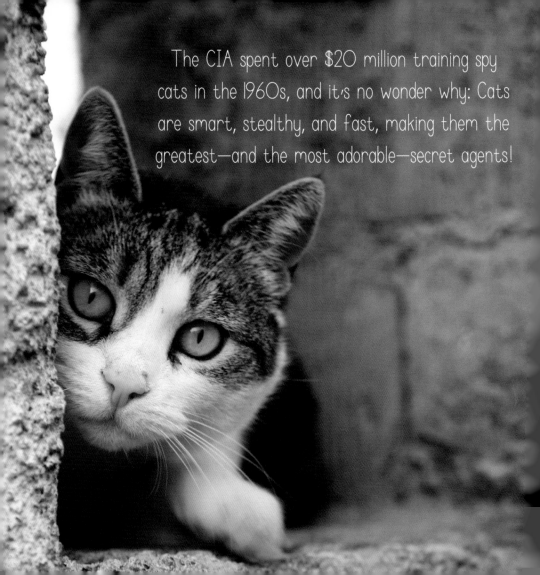

The CIA spent over $20 million training spy cats in the 1960s, and it's no wonder why: Cats are smart, stealthy, and fast, making them the greatest—and the most adorable—secret agents!